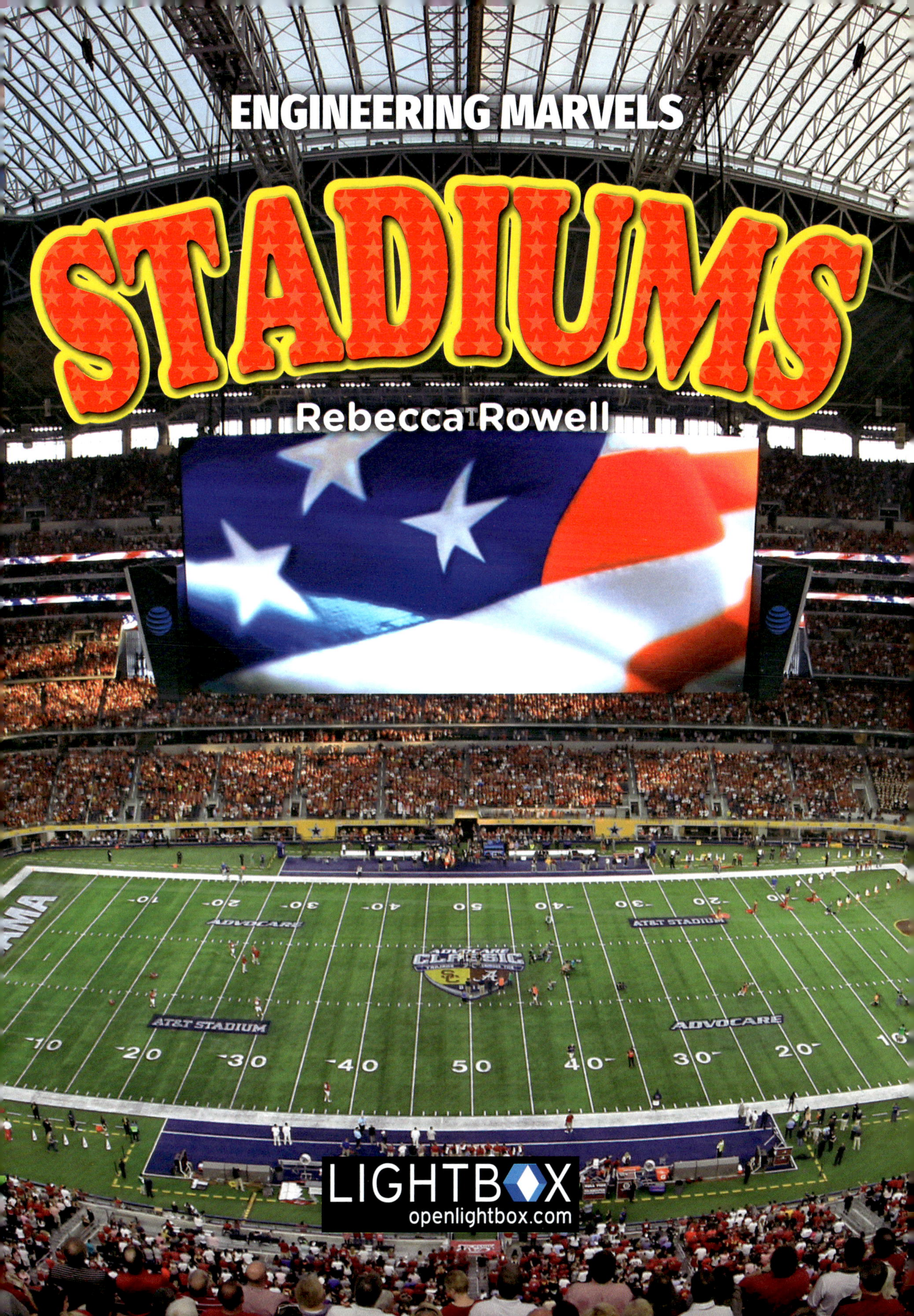

ENGINEERING MARVELS
STADIUMS
Rebecca Rowell
LIGHTBOX
openlightbox.com

Lightbox is an all-inclusive digital solution for the teaching and learning of curriculum topics in an original, groundbreaking way. Lightbox is based on National Curriculum Standards.

STANDARD FEATURES OF LIGHTBOX

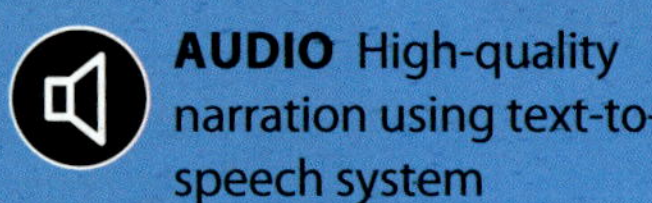

AUDIO High-quality narration using text-to-speech system

ACTIVITIES Printable PDFs that can be emailed and graded

SLIDESHOWS Pictorial overviews of key concepts

VIDEOS Embedded high-definition video clips

WEBLINKS Curated links to external, child-safe resources

TRANSPARENCIES Step-by-step layering of maps, diagrams, charts, and timelines

INTERACTIVE MAPS Interactive maps and aerial satellite imagery

QUIZZES Ten multiple choice questions that are automatically graded and emailed for teacher assessment

KEY WORDS Matching key concepts to their definitions

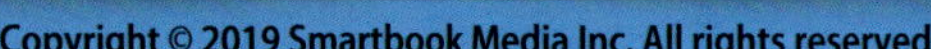
Copyright © 2019 Smartbook Media Inc. All rights reserved.

Contents

Lightbox Access Code 2

Chapter 1

A Sight to Behold 5

Chapter 2

Thoughtful Design,
Great Stadiums 10

Chapter 3

Facing Technical
Challenges.........................19

Chapter 4

Golden 1 Center 23

Mapping Stadiums........... 24

Timeline 25

Build a Stadium................ 26

Quiz 29

Key Words 30

Index................................ 31

www.openlightbox.com.. 32

Chapter 1

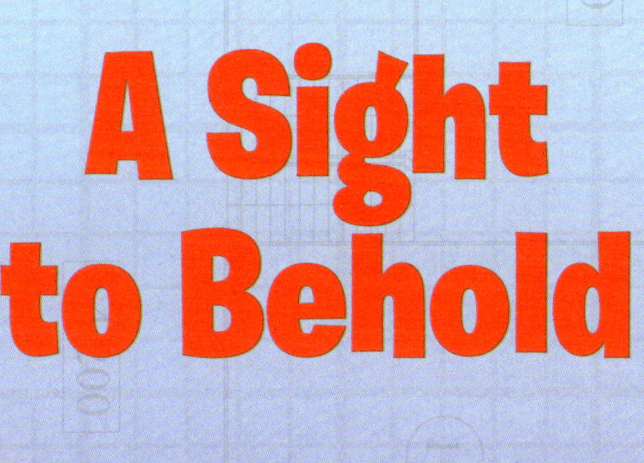

A Sight to Behold

Fans could not believe their eyes. After two years of construction, U.S. Bank Stadium in Minneapolis, Minnesota, opened to the public. Now it was time to watch a Minnesota Vikings football game. At 270 feet (82 meters) tall, the stadium towered over fans. A huge glass wall greeted visitors at the main entrance.

The 66,200-seat U.S. Bank Stadium opened in the summer of 2016.

A roof kept fans protected from rain, snow, wind, and cold. But the roof still allowed light into the stadium. Fans felt like they were outdoors.

Today's stadiums are more than just places to watch sports and concerts. They are state-of-the-art structures. It hasn't always been this way, though.

Humans have built stadiums for centuries. For example, the ancient Romans built the Colosseum nearly 2,000 years ago. But its design is not outdated. Stadiums today have the same basic **footprint**.

The Colosseum is made of stone and **concrete**. Modern stadiums use concrete. Many use steel, too. Steel is a strong but relatively lightweight metal. It allows engineers to span much longer distances, such as the U.S. Bank Stadium roof.

Today, only one-third of the original Roman Colosseum is still standing.

Germany's **Allianz Arena** is covered by **2,784** inflated panels with **300,000** color-changing lights.

At the **Janguito Malucelli Eco-Stadium** in Brazil, seats dug out of a **grassy** hill can hold **6,000** soccer fans.

It took about **eight years** to build the **Roman Colosseum.** It could hold up to **80,000** spectators.

Other changes have affected the stadium experience. Comfortable chairs have replaced simple benches or earth **berms**. Most stadiums today also have lights, scoreboards, and other electronic elements. Some newer stadiums even have hotels, restaurants, and offices inside them.

Stadiums must be designed to host events. Different sports have different needs for their stadiums. But modern engineers use their skills to create structures that do more than just house sporting events.

With new features and stunning design, many of today's stadiums are just as exciting as the events that take place inside them.

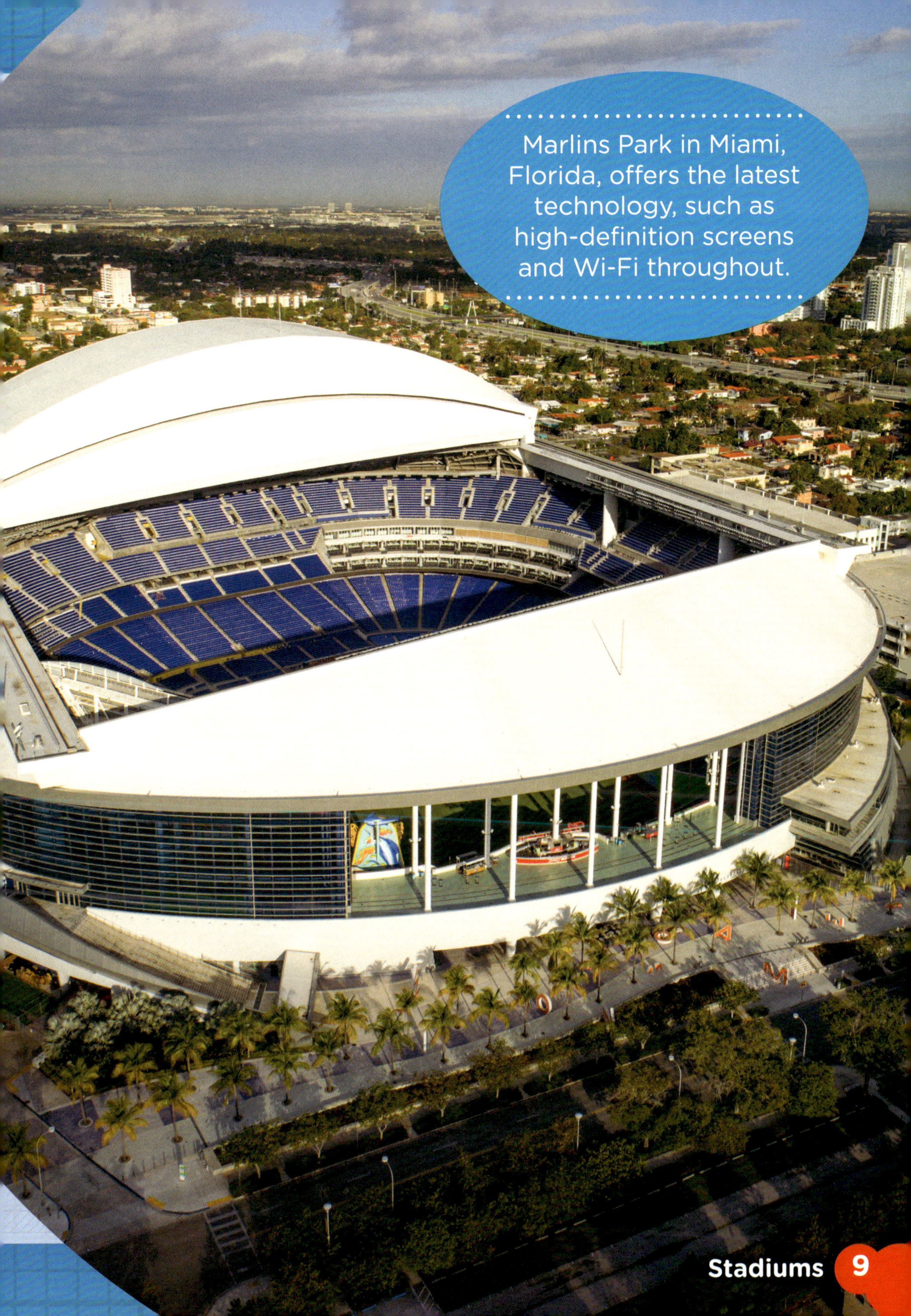

Marlins Park in Miami, Florida, offers the latest technology, such as high-definition screens and Wi-Fi throughout.

Chapter 2

Thoughtful Design, Great Stadiums

The stadium design process begins with architects. They work with the owner of the stadium to plan the basic details.

First they decide what the stadium will be used for. Then they determine its look and main features. Once the architects have a plan, the engineers help make it a reality by designing the structure.

The University of Alabama's Bryant-Denny Stadium seats more than 100,000 fans.

All stadiums must be safe. To help ensure this, engineers consider different loads. Dead load is the weight of the building itself. Floors, walls, and ceilings figure into a stadium's dead load. Live load is the weight of the items that could change over time. This includes things such as people inside the building. Environmental loads could include wind, rain, snow, and earthquakes.

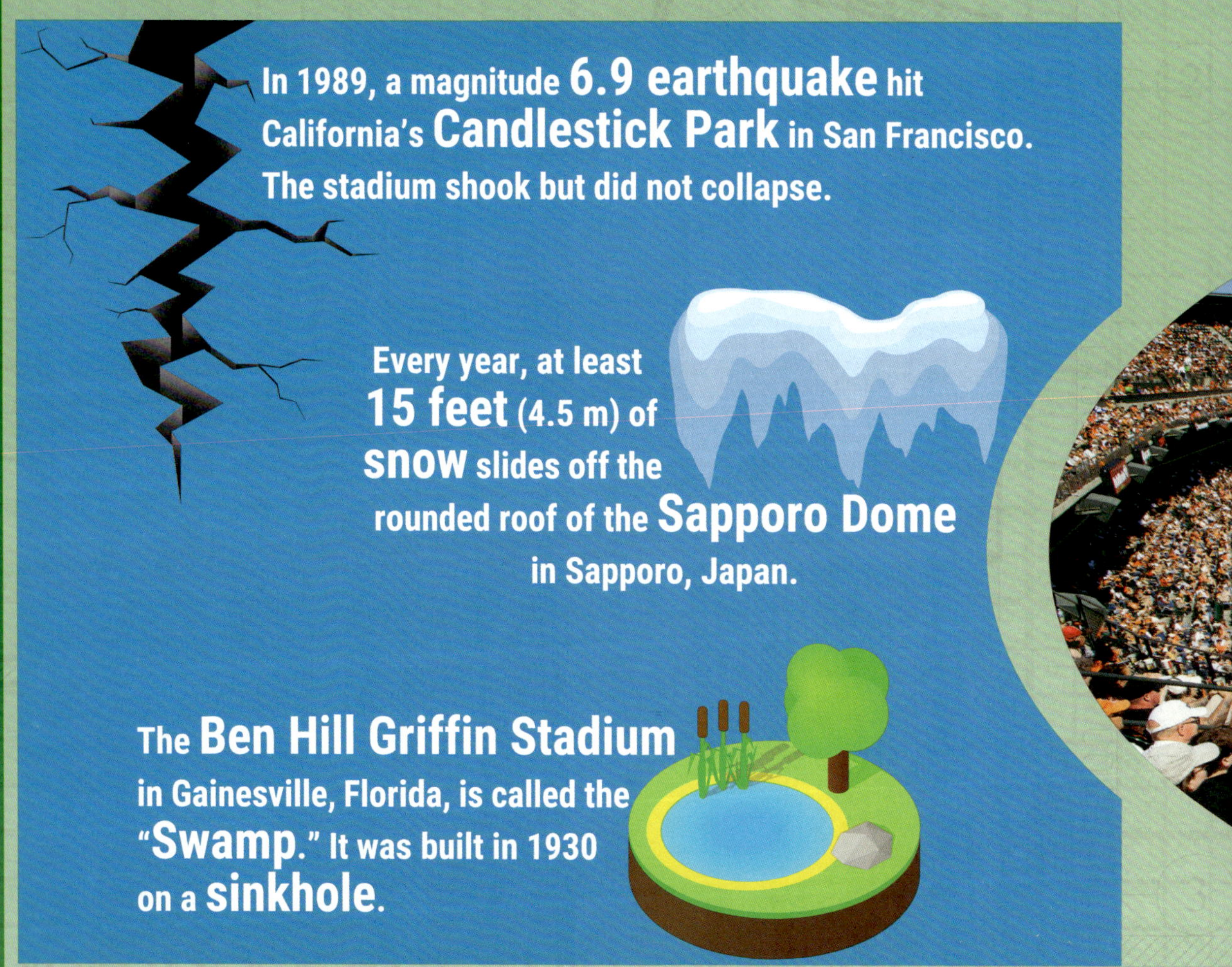

Engineers make sure the stadium is built on a firm foundation that can handle these loads. If the loads are too heavy, the soil may settle. Engineers adjust for different types of soil to prevent the stadium from settling too much.

Building codes are an important tool. These are minimum safety requirements set by a country's government. Engineers need to be familiar with these codes. They use the codes to help guide their designs.

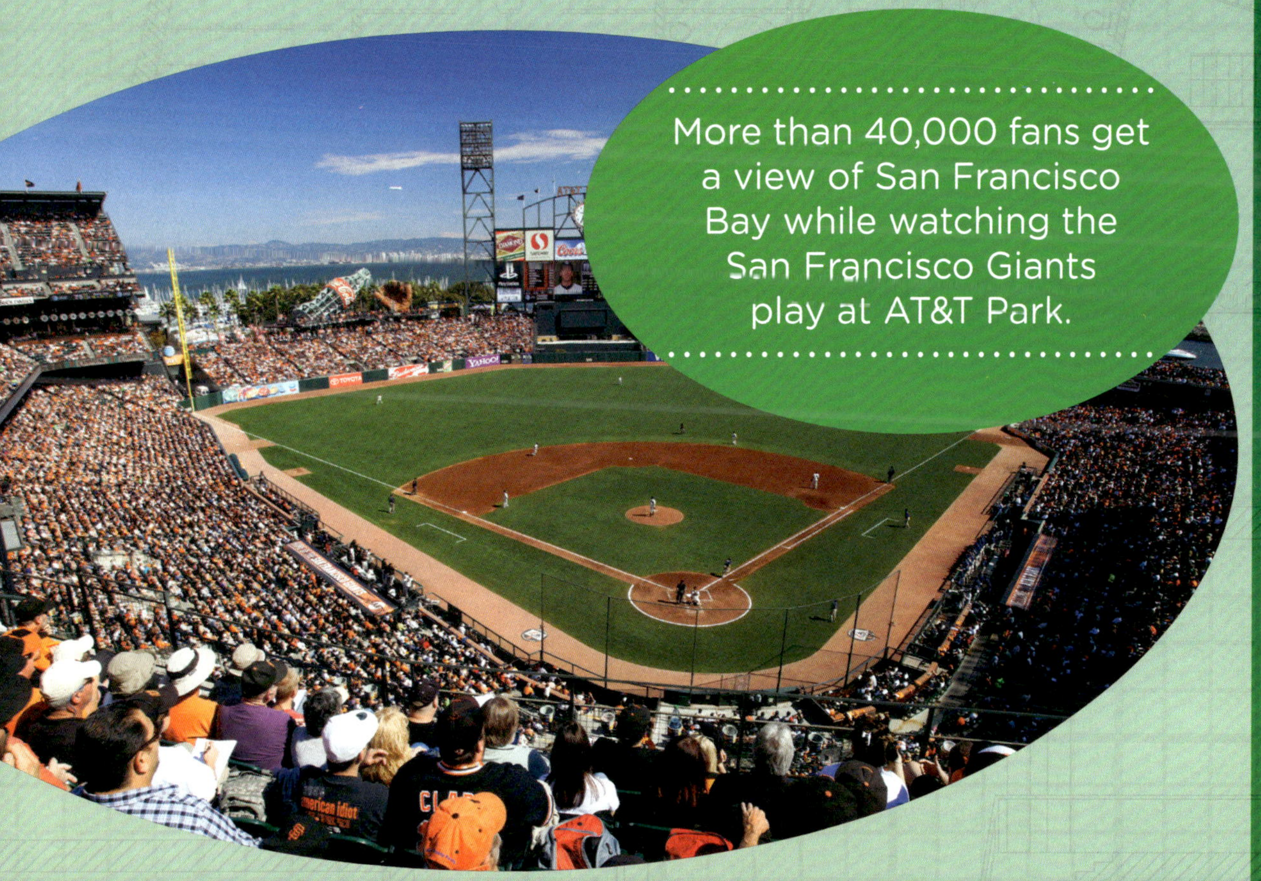

More than 40,000 fans get a view of San Francisco Bay while watching the San Francisco Giants play at AT&T Park.

Engineers select materials for a stadium. They look for materials that are strong. But they also consider cost, environment, and appearance. Wood, for example, is not as strong as concrete or steel. But it's lightweight and more affordable.

Climate affects a stadium's design. For example, many stadiums now have roofs. The roof might be flat, or it might be a dome. Some baseball and football stadiums have fully **retractable** roofs. They can be closed on cold or rainy days. Climate also influences a stadium's environmental load. In colder areas, an engineer might need to design a roof that can support snow or ice in the winter.

Builders are also making stadiums more energy **efficient**. Lincoln Financial Field in Philadelphia, Pennsylvania, is one of the most energy efficient. It has **wind turbines** and thousands of **solar panels**. These help the stadium produce its own electricity.

The Rogers Centre in Toronto, Canada, opened in 1989. It was the first stadium to have a fully retractable roof.

Money also affects some decisions. A stadium project will have a budget. Certain materials or features might need to be left out to stay on budget.

All these elements come together during the design process. The result is a stadium unlike any other. Next, workers must make the design a reality.

The 2008 Olympic Stadium in Beijing, China, was nicknamed the "Bird's Nest."

Engineering Design Process

Stadiums are complex buildings. Engineers must be confident in their plans. They use various tools and codes in their planning. This helps them make sure the final stadium meets expectations.

ASK What are the expectations for this stadium? What type of events will it host? How many people does it need to hold? What materials are needed?

IMAGINE Look at other stadiums for ideas. What ideas could be borrowed? What are some new ideas that will make this stadium stand out?

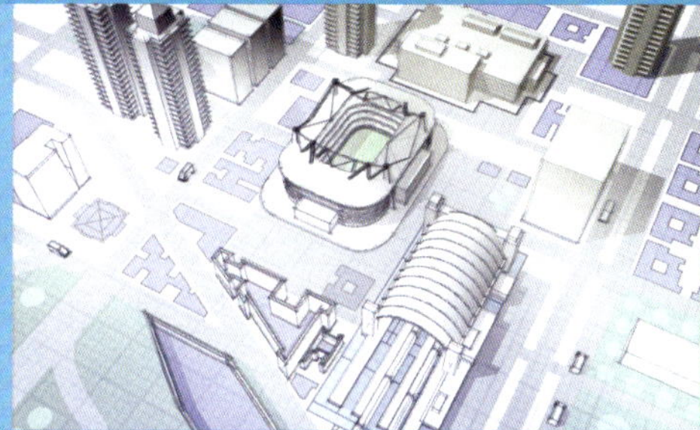

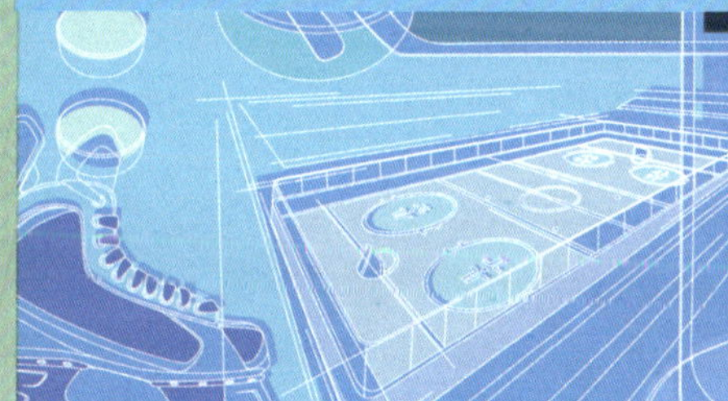

PLAN Draw a diagram. Models are also helpful.

CREATE Follow the plan and build the stadium. How does it look?

IMPROVE What works? What doesn't? What could work better? Modify the design to make it stronger.

Chapter 3

Facing Technical Challenges

Sometimes a stadium needs change. That was the case with Arthur Ashe Stadium. The tennis facility opened in 1997 in Flushing, New York. It hosts the U.S. Open each summer. However, rain often interfered with the tournament. So in 2016, a roof was added to the stadium.

New York's Arthur Ashe Stadium holds more than 23,000 people.

Adding a roof posed many challenges. Arthur Ashe Stadium was built on marshy ground. It wouldn't support a heavy roof. So engineers and architects instead designed a separate structure that would go around the existing stadium.

The structure has eight steel **columns**. They are supported by **piles** driven 175 feet (53 m) underground. This holds up the roof. The roof includes two panels. The panels each weigh 500 tons (454 metric tons). But they can open and close. The panels move on wheels set in rails. Cables pull the panels open. Fully opening the panels takes approximately seven minutes.

The roof is helpful during rainy weather. But enclosing the stadium presents a problem. Condensation forms quickly. To keep water from dripping on people in the stadium, workers installed a cooling system. Machines send cool air through a **duct**. The cool air helps prevent condensation.

Adding the roof structure to Arthur Ashe Stadium cost $150 million.

Chapter 4

The Golden 1 Center is not only a place for sports, but also for monster truck rallies, concerts, and other events.

Golden 1 Center

The Sacramento Kings basketball team moved into Golden 1 Center in 2016. When creating the venue, electrical engineers had visitors in mind. The stadium has more than 1,000 Wi-Fi hotspots. The hotspots provide Wi-Fi and cellular coverage for more than 1 million square feet (92,900 sq. m). Workers installed more than 300 miles (483 kilometers) of copper wire as well as 650 miles (1,046 km) of fiber-optic cable to power this system. The stadium even has a data center.

Golden 1 Center's technology also includes audio and visual elements. Twenty-four speakers provide surround sound. Sports fans can watch replays on a screen measuring 84 feet (26 m).

Mapping Stadiums

There are almost 900 stadiums in the United States. The map shows where a few of these engineering marvels are found. Are there any popular stadiums near you?

Michigan Stadium
Ann Arbor, Michigan
Capacity: 107,601

Michigan Stadium, nicknamed "The Big House," is the largest stadium in the United States. It was also the first stadium to use electronic scoreboards.

AT&T Stadium
Arlington, Texas
Capacity: 80,000

Home of the Dallas Cowboys, AT&T Stadium is a modern retractable-roof stadium. It opened in 2009. At that time, its high-definition video screen was the largest in the world.

Fenway Park
Boston, Massachusetts
Capacity: 37,673

Construction of Fenway Park was completed in 1912. Although it is not one of the biggest stadiums, it is the oldest U.S. baseball stadium still in use today.

UNITED STATES

Atlantic Ocean

Pacific Ocean

1

2

3

Hawai'i

100 Miles
0 161 Kilometers

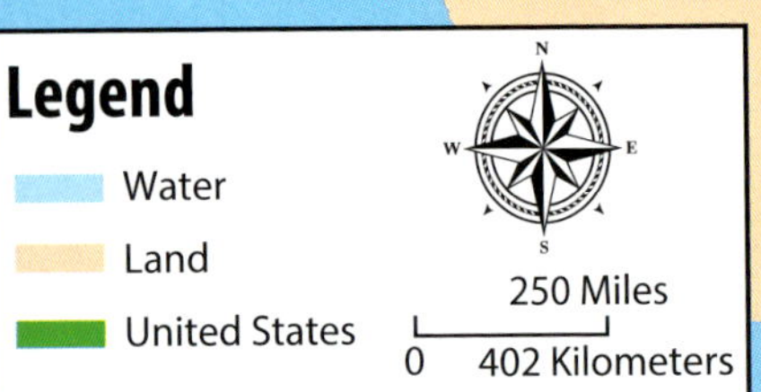

Timeline

Every year, millions of people attend all kinds of sporting events in the United States. Stadiums are designed not just to hold fans, but to add to the excitement. Discover more about the history of stadiums in the United States.

1922

Construction of the Rose Bowl in California is completed. The Rose Bowl soon becomes home to a popular college football game every year on January 1 and goes on to host five Super Bowls.

1930

Notre Dame Stadium's construction is complete. It quickly becomes one of the most popular college football stadiums. Since the 1960s, every home game but two has been a sellout.

1965

The Houston Astrodome in Texas, the first domed sports stadium, opens its doors.

1975

The Superdome is completed in New Orleans, Louisiana. At the time, it was the largest domed structure in the world.

2013

Fans at Seattle's CenturyLink Field set a world record for the loudest roar in a sports stadium. That same year, the record is broken by Kansas City Chiefs fans at Arrowhead Stadium in Kansas City, Missouri.

2028

The Los Angeles Memorial Coliseum will host its third Summer Olympic Games. It previously hosted games in 1932 and 1984.

Build a Stadium

Stadiums have many different kinds of roofs. Using strips of paper, build a colorful roof for your own shoebox stadium.

Materials

You'll need a shoebox, construction paper, and some scissors. You can add additional decorations if you'd like.

Procedure

1. Remove the lid from your shoebox. Pretend the open shoebox is an open-air stadium. But the stadium's owner wants to add a roof.

2. Cut the construction paper into narrow strips. They should be about 1 inch (2.5 centimeters) wide.

3. Place the paper strips over the shoebox to create a colorful roof for your stadium. Consider different designs. Try to come up with a roof that is both sturdy and unique.

Considerations

There are many different types of roofs. Do you want yours to be fully or partially enclosed? Should it be flat or rounded? How much natural light should it let in?

A roof needs to be sturdy. Does yours stay together on its own?

Improve It!

Are there stronger designs you can create with your paper strips?

What happens if you include wider strips of paper in your design? Try folding them. How can folded paper improve your design?

Have a friend blow against the roof as hard as he or she can. Did the roof stay standing? If not, improve it.

Try setting your scissors on the roof. Is the roof strong enough to hold the scissors?

Quiz

1. How many years did it take to construct the U.S. Bank Stadium in Minnesota?

2. What are modern stadiums made of?

3. How long did it take to build the Roman Colosseum?

4. In stadiums, what have replaced simple benches and earth berms?

5. With whom does the stadium design process begin?

6. Are floors, walls, and ceilings part of a stadium's dead load?

7. Did the 1989 earthquake cause California's Candlestick Park to collapse?

8. How long does it take to open the roof of Arthur Ashe Stadium?

9. Which is the oldest U.S. baseball stadium still in use today?

10. What year did the first domed stadium open its doors?

Answers

1. Two **2.** Concrete and steel **3.** About eight years **4.** Comfortable chairs **5.** Architects **6.** Yes **7.** No **8.** Seven minutes **9.** Fenway Park **10.** 1965

Key Words

berms: raised mounds of land

columns: vertical posts that support horizontal objects such as floors and roofs

concrete: a strong, stone-like material made from gravel, sand, cement, and water

duct: a metal tube used to carry air

efficient: accomplishing as much as possible with as little effort or resources as possible

footprint: the shape and size of the area covered or affected by an object or structure, such as a building

piles: structural elements that are driven into the ground to reach stronger soil than is available at the surface

retractable: able to be moved

solar panels: tools that convert sunlight into electricity

wind turbines: structures that create electricity from the wind

Index

architects 10, 11, 20
Arthur Ashe Stadium 19, 20, 21, 29

codes 13, 17
Colosseum 6, 7, 29
concrete 6, 14

dead loads 12, 29

engineers 6, 8, 11, 12, 13, 14, 17, 20, 23
environmental loads 12, 14

foundations 13

Golden 1 Center 22, 23

Lincoln Financial Field 14
live loads 12

materials 14, 16, 17
Minnesota Vikings 5

retractable roofs 14, 15, 19, 20
roofs 6, 14, 26, 28

Sacramento Kings 23
solar panels 14
steel 6, 14, 20, 29

U.S. Bank Stadium 5, 6, 29

Wi-Fi 9, 23
wind turbines 14

LIGHTBOX

SUPPLEMENTARY RESOURCES

Click on the plus icon found in the bottom left corner of each spread to open additional teacher resources.

- Download and print the book's quizzes and activities
- Access curriculum correlations
- Explore additional web applications that enhance the Lightbox experience

LIGHTBOX DIGITAL TITLES

Packed full of integrated media

VIDEOS

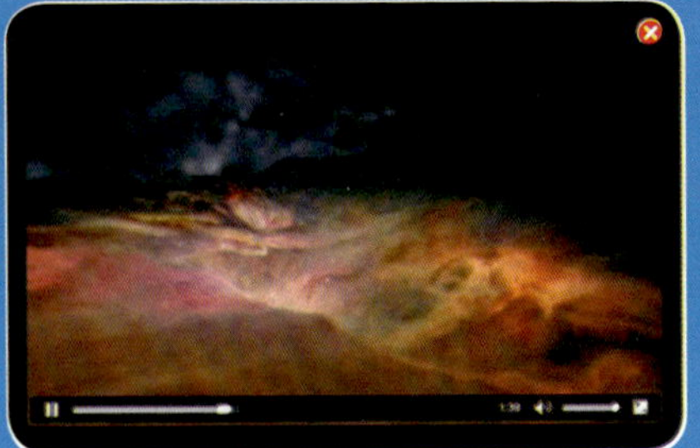

INTERACTIVE MAPS

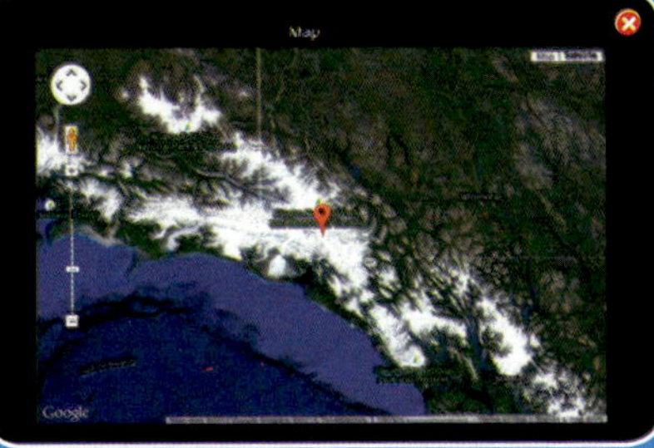

WEBLINKS

SLIDESHOWS

QUIZZES

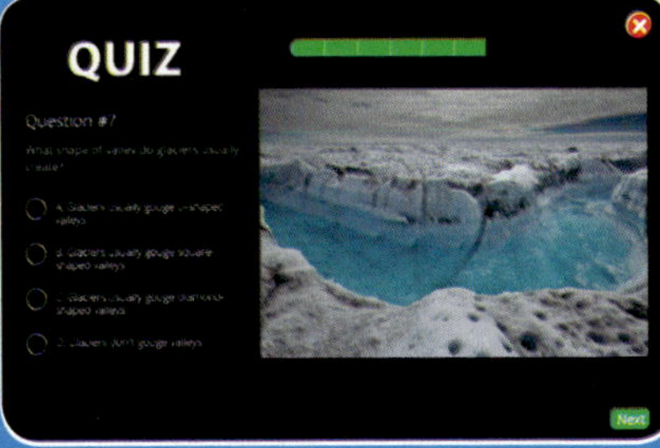

OPTIMIZED FOR

- ✓ TABLETS
- ✓ WHITEBOARDS
- ✓ COMPUTERS
- ✓ AND MUCH MORE!

Published by Smartbook Media Inc.
350 5th Avenue, 59th Floor New York, NY 10118
Website: www.openlightbox.com

Copyright © 2019 Smartbook Media Inc.
All rights reserved. No part of this publication may be reproduced, stored in a retrieval system, or transmitted in any form or by any means, electronic, mechanical, photocopying, recording, or otherwise, without the prior written permission of the publisher.

012018
151217

Library of Congress Control Number: 2017961995

ISBN 978-1-5105-3738-5 (hardcover)
ISBN 978-1-5105-3739-2 (multi-user eBook)

Printed in the Brainerd, Minnesota, United States
1 2 3 4 5 6 7 8 9 0 22 21 20 19 18

First published by North Star Editions in 2018.

Project Coordinator: Jared Siemens
Designer: Ana María Vidal

Every reasonable effort has been made to trace ownership and to obtain permission to reprint copyright material. The publisher would be pleased to have any errors or omissions brought to its attention so that they may be corrected in subsequent printings.

The publisher acknowledges Alamy, Dreamstime, Getty Images, iStock, and Shutterstock as the primary image suppliers for this title.